OUR WORLD

FRANCE

OUR WORLD

FRANCE

by Vivian Werner

Illustrated with photographs

Published by Julian Messner, a Division of Simon & Schuster, Inc.
1 West 39 Street, New York, N.Y. 10018.

Printed in the United States of America
ISBN 0-671-32429-2 Cloth Trade
ISBN 0-671-32430-6 MCE

Library of Congress Catalog Card No. 78-154972

DESIGNED BY LEON KOTKOFSKY

CONTENTS

GREAT BRITAIN
BELGIUM
LUXEMBOURG
WEST GERMANY
E. GER.
SWITZERLAND
ITALY
SPAIN
ANDORRA
MONACO
CORSICA
ENGLISH CHANNEL (La Manche)
ATLANTIC OCEAN
Bay of Biscay
MEDITERRANEAN SEA
NORMANDY
ALSACE
JURA MTS.
ALPS
PYRENEES
BASQUES
RIVIERA
Somme R.
Seine R.
Loire R.
Garonne R.
Rhône R.
Meuse R.
Rhine R.
Dunkirk
Lille
Le Havre
Rouen
Reimes
Paris
Brest
Rennes
Metz
Nancy
Strasbourg
Bonn
Orleans
St. Nazaire
Nantes
Dijon
Bern
La Rochelle
Limoges
Clermont-Ferrand
Lyons
St. Etienne
Grenoble
Milan
Bordeaux
Bayonne
Lacq
Toulouse
Nimes
Les Baux
Nice
Marseilles
Toulon
Bastia
Ajaccio
Barcelona
VINEYARDS
CATTLE
SHEEP
Map by Jaber
0 100 200
scale of miles
FRANCE
LEGEND
U⊗ uranium mining
C⊗ coal mining
CU⊗ copper mining
G⊗ gold mining
fishing
shipyards
petroleum
natural gas
primary agricultural region
hydroelectric power
nuclear power plant
chemicals
heavy metals industries
oil refinery
machinery
automobiles
textiles

1: Bastille Day

Bands are blaring, flags are flying! The very air seems alive with excitement. This is France, and today—the Fourteenth of July—is Bastille Day, the national holiday.

In every town and city, the public buildings are decorated with the colors of the country: blue, white, and red. Here, a group of people talk about the marvelous display of fireworks which will light the sky at night. There, another group sings "The Marseillaise," the national anthem:

> Come! Sons and daughters of France!
> Your day of glory is here!

Everywhere, French of all ages gather for the parades which mark the day. The most colorful of these takes place in

Paris, the capital of France. It passes down the Champs-Élysées, the widest street in the world.

On Bastille Day, every lamppost on the Champs-Élysées is decorated with bright bunting. Long before dawn, thousands of people begin to gather there. Many are native Frenchmen, but just as many are foreign tourists.

By nine o'clock, the sidewalks are crowded with men, women, and children craning their necks to get a good view. At last a cheer goes up! The *Garde Républicaine* has appeared.

The troops of the Garde are dressed in splendid uniforms of black, scarlet, and white, trimmed with gleaming gold. They wear plumed helmets, too, which seem to blaze in the sun. Sitting on magnificent black horses, the Garde slowly circles the Arch of Triumph, which stands at the top of the

The Bastille Day parade marches down the Champs-Élysées and passes in front of the Arch of Triumph.

Champs-Élysées. Today, the Arch is hung with a huge *tricolor*—the three-colored French flag.

After the Garde, the first brass band in the parade marches down the avenue. It is followed by paratroopers, wearing their red berets at a jaunty angle. Ski troops come next, dressed all in white and balancing white skis on their shoulders. Tanks, landing craft, and trucks, carrying guns and rockets, rumble past the crowds. Then swaying camels plod along, ridden by the white-robed, hooded soldiers who serve in desert wars.

Finally planes fly overhead, trailing blue, white, and red smoke. The planes soon disappear, but the streaks of smoke hang in the sky. When they float together, they form the largest *tricolor* of all, high above the crowd.

On Bastille Day, the people of France celebrate the beginning of the French Revolution. It was on that day they took their first steps toward democracy. Thousands of them who lived in Paris rose against their king on July 14, 1789, and demanded the right to govern themselves.

They seized guns and cannons. Then they marched to the Bastille, a fortress which was used as a prison. There they climbed the walls and broke down the doors. Once inside the Bastille, the angry citizens freed the prisoners of the king. From then on, the motto of the French was "*Liberté, égalite, fraternité*"—liberty, equality, brotherhood.

When they chose their slogan, the French had the American Declaration of Independence in mind. In the Declaration, the colonists boldly stated that every citizen had the right to life, liberty, and the pursuit of happiness. One of the leaders of the French Revolution, the Marquis de Lafayette, had helped the Americans to win those rights, fighting at the side of George Washington.

Many of the French people who watch the Bastille Day parade today are opposed to the ideals for which Lafayette fought. Many would even like to see a king rule France again. They do not believe that all men are equal, and they feel that such an idea has cost them many of the privileges they themselves won through the Revolution. Such Frenchmen are usually the prosperous businessmen, doctors, law-

The capture of the Bastille, as shown in an early French drawing.

yers, and other professional people who form the social class known as the *bourgeoisie.* They dream of France as it was, long ago.

Another class of Frenchmen dreams of a better future. They are the students, professors, writers, and artists—the intellectuals who contribute to the culture of their country. They are greatly respected for the books they write and the pictures they paint. But they are also respected because they are so often in the forefront of the fight for justice.

These intellectuals celebrate Bastille Day at *bals*—street dances. Wherever one is held, the chestnut trees are draped with strings of paper lanterns, as well as blue, white, and red lights. The dancing goes on for three nights, the thirteenth, fourteenth, and fifteenth of July, while bands play popular waltzes, sambas, or the great French favorite, American jazz.

There is a third type of celebration in Paris on Bastille Day. This is a fair or carnival. Ferris wheels, merry-go-rounds, and roller coasters are set up. There are shooting galleries and wheels of fortune, too. Scattered among them are stands from which you can buy delicious sugar-sprinkled waffles or thin pancakes spread with jam.

The largest, liveliest, and noisiest of the fairs is the one at the Place de la Bastille, where the old fortress once stood. There the members of the working class of Paris gather. They are maids, carpenters, salesgirls, and delivery boys, all dressed in clean but threadbare clothes. On Bastille Day they have just one thing in mind: to forget the drudgery and

Celebrating Bastille Day at a *bal* in Paris.

poverty of their daily lives and enjoy themselves for the moment.

When they meet their friends, they stop at a café and share a pitcher of strong red wine. As they drink, they talk about how difficult life is for them. They say they work too long and earn too little. They want a better life.

They do not look to the past like the wealthy bourgeoisie. They cannot wait for the future like the intellectuals. Instead, they think of the present, and many of them even talk of another revolution.

So France today is divided. It is not the first time that this has been so. Nearly two thousand years ago, the great Roman general, Julius Caesar, wrote about Gaul as France was then called. He described it in a famous sentence: "All Gaul is divided into three parts." That is as true today as it was in ancient times.

Even on Bastille Day, the national holiday, classes never mix or mingle. Everyone observes Bastille Day but in the way of his own class. The French do not yet have the equality and brotherhood which they celebrate.

2:

In the Early Days

In 1951, Paris celebrated a birthday. The city was two thousand years old!

It was founded by the Parisii, one of the hundreds of tribes of Gaul. Most of the other tribes were roving bands of robbers and murderers, who lived on what they plundered. The Parisii, though, were traders. They sailed the River Seine, which flows through the heart of France. To protect themselves from pirates lurking on the shores, they built their huts on an island in the Seine, and surrounded them with fortifications. Today their settlement bears their name, Paris.

More than a hundred years before the birth of Christ, Roman soldiers appeared in Gaul. They came to help those tribes battling the Gauls, but they stayed to open trade routes. Before long, some of them settled on the land. Then, about 47 B.C., Julius Caesar, the Roman Emperor, conquered the scattered tribes of Gaul and became their master.

The Romans built fortifications, as well as arenas, roads, and aqueducts. They were fine engineers, and many of their works still stand.

Christianity was brought to Gaul by the Romans. They introduced their language, Latin, to the tribes, too. But over the years, the Gauls gradually changed the language. Now it is French, a different, but similar, tongue.

The conquerors passed laws and judged everyone according to them. This idea of judgment according to law is still

An arena built by the Romans which still stands in the city of Arles.

the basis of justice in the Western world. Above all, the Romans set up a system of government, headed by a strong official who appointed those serving under him.

When trouble broke out in Italy, their own land, the Roman soldiers and officials returned to it. They left no strong leader behind them, and the Gauls did not know how to maintain law and order. Soon the old tribes were fighting one another again.

Then hordes of barbarians invaded Gaul, attracted by her rich soil and mild climate. One tribe, the Franks, which came from Germany, gave the country its present name, France.

Eight hundred years after Julius Caesar first brought civilization to France, one of her kings restored civilization to the country. His name was Charlemagne, meaning "Charles the Great."

Charlemagne admired Caesar and copied him wherever possible. He followed Roman customs and enforced Roman laws. And he organized a government much like theirs.

Charlemagne was such a devout Christian that the Pope himself crowned him in the year 800. He was given the title "Emperor of all the Romans." For a while, there was peace and prosperity in the land. The great monastic orders were founded then; they survive to this day. And the first of the great cathedrals, which are still the glory of France, were begun.

But after Charlemagne, the kings of France were weak. They could not protect their subjects, and so the people

The crowning of Charlemagne.

turned to those who could—the nobles who were the great landowners.

These nobles permitted the people to build their homes on their property, and to take shelter within the walls of their castles in times of danger. In return, the people tilled the lands of the nobles, provided them with all their needs, and gave them complete allegiance. This system, feudalism, lasted many years.

But the constant warfare between the nobles, in feudal days, meant starvation and death for the workers and peasants. Foreign wars added to their misery. The war which broke out in 1337 between France and England went on for more than a century. During that time, much of France was conquered by the English.

The rest of the country would have fallen, too, if it had not been for the courage of a sixteen-year-old farm girl, Joan of Arc.

One day, as Joan watched her sheep, she heard voices speaking to her. God, they said, had chosen her to save her country. She must go at once to the Dauphin, Charles VII, the crown prince of France.

But the Dauphin's palace was hundreds of miles away, and Joan had never before left her village. Nearby, though, was a royal garrison. Joan sought out the captain and poured out her story.

He scoffed at first, but the young girl's faith was so great that she soon convinced even that hardheaded officer of her mission. He ordered her to change her rough peasant dress for man's clothes, and then escorted her to the Dauphin.

Charles, a weak and frightened man, took heart when Joan knelt before him and hailed him "on behalf of the Great Lord" as king of France. He provided her with a suit of armor and what arms he could spare, along with the few troops at his command.

Time after time, Joan led her pathetic little army into battle. She rode at their head, carrying the banner specially made for her. It was the red silk battle flag of the kings of France, with their insignia, the *fleur-de-lys*, embroidered on one flame-shaped streamer, and Joan's own motto "Jesus

Joan of Arc leading her followers at the battle of Orléan.

Maria" on the other. The sight of Joan's banner gave the raggle-taggle army a courage that more than made up for their lack of arms and training.

Joan won victory after victory, and as a result the Dauphin could at last claim the title of king. He was crowned in the cathedral at Rheims, in 1429, while Joan stood by, holding high her banner.

The war went on, though, and Joan was captured by the English. She was tried for witchcraft, and when she refused to retract her story of the voices, she was sentenced to death. She was burned at the stake on May 30, 1431, when she was nineteen years old. But her men fought on, and thanks to their faith in Joan, they drove the English out of France and united the country. Today, the young peasant girl is honored as Saint Joan, the savior of France.

In the years that followed, France again prospered. There were times of trouble, but they were short. Usually the troubles were over religion. As in other lands, Catholics and Protestants fought over the way they should worship.

Although there were wars with other countries, they were fought on foreign soil. Moreover, the French armies were made up entirely of professional soldiers, who were paid to do the fighting.

The people of France were safe at last. The peasants stayed home to farm their lands and often became rich. Cities were safe, and so they grew. There was time for learning, and schools and universities were established.

The kings of France did their best for their country and their people. Most of them devoted their time to good works, and let their ministers govern the country. But they chose wise men as ministers.

In the year 1643, a five-year-old boy, Louis XIV, became king of France! It was many years before he was old enough to govern, and until that time, his mother took his place. But as he grew older, Louis made up his mind that he, and he alone, would rule his country. "The State—I am the State," he said.

Louis XIV looked for intelligent men to advise him, and he found them in every country, in every walk of life. With their help, industries were started, farming was expanded, and trade was increased. Frenchmen had already explored parts of the New World. Now they pushed deeper and Father

The Sun King, Louis XIV.

Marquette, in Canada, reached the Great Lakes. The Cavalier de la Salle sailed down the Mississippi and claimed the whole region for France. He called it Louisiana, in honor of his king.

French armies spread through Europe and conquered territories. But they suffered severe defeats, too. The upkeep of his armies sent Louis deeply into debt. His one great folly, though, was not his costly wars but his denial of religious liberty to the Huguenots, the French Protestants. As a result, hundreds of thousands of the most skilled and gifted Frenchmen left the country.

Louis continued to live in splendor in the great palace he built at Versailles, near Paris. There he was surrounded by the most beautiful women of France and the most distinguished noblemen. He entertained them all lavishly. But he also brought to his court the great thinkers of this time. Among them were poets, musicians, philosophers, and playwrights, whose ideas have influenced the entire world.

Every king in Europe knew of the glory of Versailles. They copied the fashions set by Louis XIV and tried to make their own courts the equal of his. But none ever did.

The court at Versailles was so brilliant that Louis XIV was called the Sun King. The time in which he ruled was the greatest in the history of France.

3: One—Two—Three—Four—Five Republics

The luxuries of the court of Versailles had to be paid for, and it was the poor people of France who bore the cost. They were taxed more and more, to provide funds for the glittering balls at which Louis XIV entertained, and for the jewels and castles he gave his friends.

Louis's descendants were as extravagant as he had been. None was worse than his great-grandson, Louis XVI. He spent money lavishly, with no thought of his subjects, although most of them lived in hovels, dressed in rags, and often went without food.

At last the French workers were so poor they could pay no more. The upper classes, though, were prosperous. Moreover, they enjoyed a special privilege: they paid no taxes at all. Louis XVI decided the time had come for them to do so.

He called together representatives of the church, the aristocracy, and the wealthy middle class, and asked them to give up their ancient right of tax exemption. Under feudal law, it was their duty to obey this command of the king.

But the assembled representatives were tired of feudalism. They had learned about democracy from the philosophers who had been at the courts of Louis XIV and Louis XV. So the representatives ignored their monarch's request and asked to govern themselves. They even asked for a constitution, like that in America.

The king refused to listen to them and called out his troops. When the news reached Paris, the citizens seized arms and marched to the Bastille. It was on that day July 14, 1789, that the Revolution began. It lasted for ten years.

The king quickly gave in to the citizens and granted them a constitution. It provided for a parliament through which he would rule. But the people were not content.

Soon they turned against the royal family and the nobility. They put thousands of them to death. Among the victims were Louis XVI and his queen, Marie Antoinette.

The people turned against the Catholic Church, too, which had become rich and powerful. Church leaders were executed, and church property was destroyed.

In 1792, France was proclaimed a republic, but the bloodshed went on. The leaders of the Revolution were suspicious of everyone and especially of each other. So one after another was executed. The people lived in such fear that those days were called "The Terror." They ended only with the death of Robespierre, the man responsible for much of the cruelty.

By then France was desperate. There was no work, and people were cold and hungry. Even worse, the old wars started by the kings to annex other countries were still going on. New wars had also broken out when European royalty, fearing that the revolution might spread, attacked France.

Yet there was good news from those battlefields where a young general, Napoléon Bonaparte, won victory after victory. He kept an eye on events at home, too, and when France seemed on the verge of another revolution, he hurried to Paris. There, in 1799, Napoléon proclaimed himself ruler of France.

Napoléon, like Charlemagne, admired and copied Julius Caesar. Therefore, he called himself "First Consul," after Caesar's title.

He, too, reorganized France and set up a strong government which he headed. He divided the country into districts or *départements*. Each was headed by a *préfet*. Moreover, he classified all the laws of the country in a system called the Code Napoléon. It is still used in France and much of Europe.

Under Napoléon, France recovered from the destruction of the Revolution. The people were well-off, and the general was so popular that he was named First Consul for life. In

Napoléon Bonaparte, the general who made himself Emperor of France.

1804, the French made Napoléon their Emperor. He was crowned in the great cathedral of Notre-Dame in Paris.

The wars went on. Napoléon's armies sent home enough treasure to make France rich. And they conquered almost every country in Europe, one after the other.

But the other nations at last united against the Emperor. Together, they defeated him, and in 1815 he was sent into exile. The French, who had lost hundreds of thousands of men, were sick of the slaughter and glad to see Napoléon go.

For the next fifty years, France tried different forms of government. First, the kings were brought back. They gave their subjects very little more liberty than Louis XIV or Louis XVI had. Otherwise, they were far different from those monarchs.

They avoided war whenever possible. They lived modestly. Instead of surrounding themselves with brilliant and clever people, they spent their time with down-to-earth businessmen.

Under the last of these kings, Louis-Philippe, grants of money were given to businessmen to build factories and to install the new machines which were the marvels of the age. Factory products were shipped throughout France on the railroads which had just been built. New markets were opened up by the establishment of a French colony in Algeria, on the coast of North Africa.

France had never before been so prosperous. But Louis-Philippe was unpopular, and in 1848 he was overthrown in a revolution. That same year, Louis Napoléon, the nephew of Napoléon Bonaparte, was elected first president of the Second Republic.

Louis Napoléon was as ambitious as his uncle. On December 2, 1851, he took complete control of the French government, arresting his opponents and dissolving the Assembly. A few weeks later, he was re-elected President of France. And on December 2, 1852, just one year after he had seized full power, he was made Emperor of France by popular vote. He called himself Napoléon III.

Like Louis-Philippe's government, Napoléon's lent funds to great industrialists, helping them to build more railroads. Coal mines were dug, harbors were dredged, and docks were built. Ships were constructed, too, while French factories grew in number. Finally the Suez Canal was built in Egypt, making it possible to ship French goods to the Far East.

Napoléon III soon added new colonies to the French possessions. Among them were New Caledonia in the Pacific, Indochina in Southeast Asia, and Morocco and Tunisia in North Africa.

At home, schools and hospitals were built. Old-age pensions were introduced, and workers were allowed to join unions, which had been forbidden under Napoléon Bonaparte.

Then, in 1870, the Franco-Prussian war broke out. Neither the Emperor nor Kaiser Wilhelm I, the ruler of Germany, wanted war. But Wilhelm's chancellor, Bismarck, did. He changed the wording of a telegram from the Kaiser to Napoléon so that it insulted the French and provoked them into declaring war. Immediately, the Prussian army invaded France, and defeated her within a few months.

The peace terms imposed on France were harsh. She had to pay a huge sum of money to the Germans. Worse, she had to give them Alsace and Lorraine, two of her richest provinces.

Bitter over their defeat, the French again overthrew the government. In its place they set up the Third Republic. It lasted until 1940.

The Third Republic was only a few months old when the people of Paris, who lacked faith in the new leaders, rose against them. In 1871, they set up their own government, the

When Paris was ruled by the Commune, the workers battled the soldiers in the city streets.

Paris Commune. Their revolt was quickly crushed, but thousands of Parisians were killed, and much of the city was destroyed.

Yet France had become so wealthy under Napoléon III that she quickly recovered. The debt to Germany was paid within a few months, and Paris was rebuilt. Raw materials from the colonies kept factory wheels spinning, and France was powerful enough to conquer new territories in Africa.

But in 1914, war broke out again between Germany and France. The cause was the assassination of an Austrian Archduke by a Serbian patriot. It was a minor incident in which neither France nor Germany was directly involved. But both countries had made treaties with a number of other nations who were involved, and they rushed to the aid of their allies. Before long, most of Europe was at war.

The fighting lasted four terrible years, and much of it took place on French soil. When it was over, France had won back Alsace and Lorraine. But she had lost hundreds of thousands of men, her cities were destroyed, and her farmlands ruined.

Germany was in an even worse state. Her people were starving, and they turned to a fanatical Austrian house painter, Adolf Hitler, for help. When he promised them "the world," they made him their *Führer* (leader).

Hitler attacked one country after another, then invaded France in 1940. Her defense system was old-fashioned, and the country collapsed in six weeks. For the next five years, much of her land was occupied by German troops.

Those were the darkest days for France since the time of Joan of Arc. Yet there was one ray of hope. A French officer who escaped to London broadcast an appeal to his countrymen to join him in freeing their land. "*Moi, Général de Gaulle*—" he began ("I, General de Gaulle"). He added, "France has lost a battle; she has not lost the war."

A French army was formed, which fought alongside those of England and America. When France was liberated in 1945, General Charles de Gaulle became president of the provisional government. He served until 1946, when the Fourth French Republic was set up.

On June 18, 1940, General de Gaulle broadcast an appeal to his countrymen, asking them to join him in freeing France.

Generous American aid helped France recover from the Second World War. But there was trouble overseas, where several colonies demanded freedom. In 1954, the French were defeated in Indochina, and that country became independent.

The struggle for the North African colony of Algeria was so bitter that it brought France close to civil war, and led to the downfall of the Fourth Republic. When a Fifth Republic was established, Charles de Gaulle was elected President.

De Gaulle freed Algeria and all the African colonies as well. Then he turned his attention to foreign affairs. By establishing good relations with West Germany, he ended forever the threat of invasions from France's neighbor.

It was de Gaulle's ambition to make France a world power again, as great as she was during the reign of Charlemagne. But he was so occupied with his dream of glory that he overlooked the discontent at home. In May, 1968, a revolt broke out against him. It was led by students demanding more and better schools. Workers, asking for higher wages and better working conditions, joined the students. The revolt paralyzed France for six weeks. It ended only when government troops surrounded Paris.

A few months later, de Gaulle asked the French people to vote for certain changes in the constitution. One change would strip the French Senate of what power it had. The second would give the *départements* more voice in the national government. When de Gaulle's proposals were rejected, he resigned. Georges Pompidou, who had been *premier*

General de Gaulle (left) and Georges Pompidou (right) who was elected to take the General's place.

(prime minister) under de Gaulle, was elected to take the General's place.

President Pompidou tries to carry out de Gaulle's plans. He also pays great attention to foreign affairs. But he has learned his lesson and is making reforms at home, too.

4: The French Government

When the French established their five republics, they drew up constitutions for them. Each constitution began with the Declaration of the Rights of Man, which states that men everywhere should enjoy liberty and equality.

The constitutions then went on to outline the forms of the French governments. In each republic, the chief executive has been a president, who is now elected by direct vote. Until recently, the president was only a figurehead. It has been the premier and the members of his cabinet who decided and directed policy.

The premier has always been appointed by the president, while cabinet members are appointed by the premier. The number of cabinet ministers varies, depending on the needs of the country at any particular time. There may be as few as twelve ministers or as many as twenty.

Some ministers have the same functions as cabinet members in the United States. One heads the Department of Justice, another the Department of Labor. But France has other ministers, like the one for Cultural Affairs, who oversees the art museums, the national theaters, and the care of the great cathedrals and other monuments.

The appointment of the premier, as well as of cabinet members, must be approved by the National Assembly. This is one of the two houses of the parliament, the legislative

The National Assembly in session.

branch of the French government. The Assembly, or Chamber of Deputies, is made up of 487 members. Deputies are elected by direct vote and stay in office five years.

The second house of the Parliament is the Senate. It has 274 members who are elected by indirect vote for nine years.

Senators serve mainly as advisers to the government, although, like the Deputies, they can introduce laws and must vote on them. But a law passed by the Senate can be voted down by the Deputies. On the other hand, if the Senate votes down a law passed by the Assembly, it still becomes law if passed by a second vote of the Assembly. Not even the president can veto a bill which the Deputies have approved, although he can ask them to reconsider it.

The Assembly is so powerful that it can force the premier and his cabinet to resign by voting a "motion of censure." If the Deputies then refuse to approve a new premier chosen by the president, the country is left without a leader.

This happened so often in the past that the Constitution of the Fifth Republic gave the president three new powers. He can now dissolve the National Assembly and order new elections. He can ask the people to vote directly on certain bills. And if the country is in danger, he can take full power for six months.

France also has a judicial branch of the government. Members of it are thought of as civil servants—public employees—like postal workers or customs inspectors in the United States. Civil servants are appointed for life. They begin their service in the lowest courts of the country, then work their way up.

A trial before a jury is held in France only for serious crimes or in civil suits of great importance. In all other cases, the verdict and the sentence are pronounced by from one to three judges. Their number depends on the importance of the case. If there is a jury, its decision need not be unanimous, as in the United States. Instead, the vote of the majority decides the outcome.

Judges and prosecutors can question witnesses, who are required to answer. The point of a trial in France is to determine the truth in any way at all. The rights of the accused are by no means protected to the extent they are in the United States.

Not only judges but hundreds of thousands of other officials belong to the civil service. Among them are tax assessors, *préfets*, and deans of universities.

The very top civil servants are those who make up the Councils of State. One Council interprets each new law, and sees that it does not violate the constitution or conflict with past laws. Another Council advises the government on the bills which should be drafted. Still a third oversees the appointment and promotion of judges. Like all civil servants, Council members are appointed for life and continue to serve even when the government changes.

The French civil service is so vast and so important that it really forms an invisible government. Civil servants run the schools where other civil servants are trained. They must attend these schools for three years, after graduating from the university. They set their own examinations, too, and make their own promotions.

By law, the schools are open to all young people. Usually, though, preference is given to friends and families of those already in the service. Many positions, therefore, are inherited rather than earned.

This is one reason why some people like Monsieur and Madame Dupont, who live in Châtillon, a small town near Paris, don't vote in national elections. "What's the use?" M. Dupont asks, shrugging his shoulders. "Nothing changes, no matter how we vote."

But M. Dupont doesn't feel that way about his local government. Châtillon is one of 38,000 *communes* (towns and villages) of France. It elects its own mayor and city council. The *département* in which Châtillon is located, like all ninety-nine *départements* in France, is headed by a *préfet*

The mayor of a small town meets with the City Council.

Counting the ballots on election day.

appointed from Paris, just as one was at the time of Napoléon. Then, though, the *préfet* was appointed by the Emperor himself; now he is chosen by the Minister of the Interior.

However, the *préfet* no longer governs the *département*; he serves as a link between the different *communes* and Paris. If Châtillon needs a new bridge or better streetlights, the *préfet* helps the mayor get them.

The mayor of Châtillon is a friend of the Duponts. They count on him to issue marriage licenses, collect local taxes, and keep law and order.

When Châtillon holds an election, M. and Mme. Dupont are sure to vote. They cast their ballots for the man they know, regardless of his party.

Most French people follow the pattern of the Duponts. Forty percent do not vote in a national election. Those who do go to the polls vote for one of the dozen political parties, rather than for the candidate himself.

Many French political parties are very small. The two largest are the Union for a Democratic Republic, which was formed by the supporters of General de Gaulle, and the Communist Party. The Communists regularly win 20 percent of the vote.

The French Communist Party is not interested in overthrowing the government but in working with it to obtain benefits for the workers. It has already succeeded in cutting their working hours, raising their hourly pay, and getting them pensions and medical care.

Moreover, in many places where the Mayor is a Communist, nurseries for the children of working mothers have been set up. Some *communes* which are governed by the Communists have gone far beyond this, and built theaters, art and sport centers complete with swimming pools for their citizens.

The Communist Party was the first group in France to organize a resistance to Adolf Hitler. Today it is the only organization which holds meetings at which voters can meet party leaders and discuss their problems. So the Communist Party in France has gained and held the respect of voters. They have greater confidence in it than in any other French political party.

5: The French People

People from all over Europe have been drawn to France for thousands of years. They came as invaders, and they came to trade. Later, immigrants came, looking for more freedom or a better life.

All belonged to different races. But they mingled and intermarried. Finally they produced a new people, the French.

Yet in some parts of the country, most people show the special traits of their ancestors. In the north, where the Norsemen settled, the French are tall, blond, and blue-eyed. They are a stern, hardworking group who waste no words. When asked a question, they grunt an answer. Such Frenchmen are cautious and stick to the tried and true. They want no part of "newfangled notions."

The people of eastern France are blond, too. But they are short and stocky, like their ancestors who once lived in the mountainous Alpine regions surrounding France. Some, who have Slavic blood in their veins, have round faces with chubby cheeks and snub noses.

The easterner is as hardworking and serious as his fellow Frenchman in the north. But he changes his ways more

These are some of the people of France.

easily and more often. When his work is done, he relaxes and enjoys life.

The French in the south are short and chunky, with dark eyes and olive-colored skin. They talk a great deal, always very fast and often very loud. They don't care who overhears them, and they will shout and argue in a crowed street without the least embarrassment.

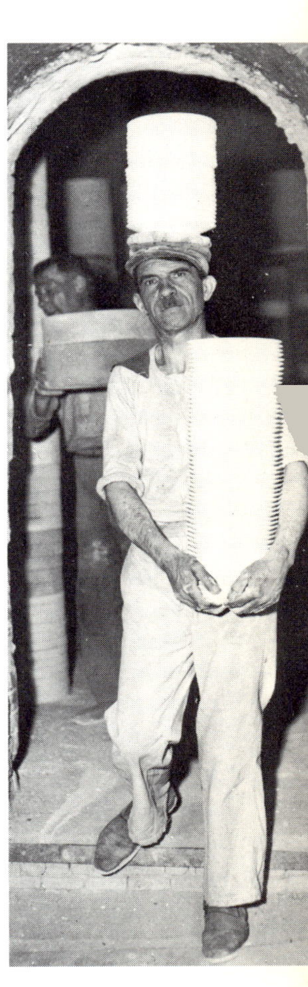

The French of the south are gay and happy, and are not afraid to show it. Their clothing is as brightly colored as the decorations in their homes. But they are temperamental and often flare in anger for little reason. Yet they quickly forget their differences, usually over a glass of the local wine.

There is friendly rivalry between the people of various regions, and especially between those who live in Paris and those who live elsewhere. Parisians think of all other Frenchmen as country bumpkins. The others, though, consider Parisians to be city slickers.

Most French are Catholics. But that doesn't mean they go to church very often. Except for children and a few devout older people, the average Frenchman goes to church only to be married or buried!

A large number of North Africans, who are Muslims, live in France. The nation also has the largest Jewish community in Europe. There are Protestants of all sects, too. No matter what their religion, all are allowed to worship freely.

The common language is French. Accents, however, may be so different that people in one part of the country have difficulty understanding people from another section. Those from the northern parts of France speak with a twang like that of the New Englander in the United States, and those in the south drawl their words, like inhabitants of Georgia or Mississippi.

The people of France have a special attitude toward life. It is one of *joie de vivre* (delight in living). It means enjoying the great books, the best in music, the most wonderful paintings and works of sculpture. But it also means enjoying life on a more simple level. It means planting flowers wherever they will grow, and arranging cut flowers with the greatest care, even in the most modest apartment. It means sitting in a café and watching the sunset, or savoring a well-prepared meal.

To all Frenchmen, cooking is an art. They love to talk about food, and they love to eat. French *chefs* (leading cooks) are famous, and people travel many miles for an especially good meal. Every housewife, too, prides herself on her cooking. Her dishes may be simple, but they are sure to be delicious.

The French housewife, like her husband, is thrifty. Often this trait is carried to an extreme. Peasants especially are well-known for pinching *sous* (pennies).

No one likes to pay taxes. But the French hate paying them so much that they are proud if they can cheat the government. Yet they expect the state to pay their medical expenses and old-age pensions, and to give them better roads and schools.

Visitors to France often find the people cold and say it is difficult to make friends with them. In reality, French people are simply so devoted to their own families that they have no time for strangers.

One word sums up the people of France: contradictory. They think clearly, yet act unreasonably. They work hard,

A school for chefs.

yet cut corners wherever possible. They are open-minded, yet suspicious.

They believe in democracy and are willing to die for that belief, but they vote dictators into office. They insist that all men should have equal rights, but each demands some special privilege for himself.

Many years ago, General de Gaulle noted these characteristics of his countrymen. He went on to describe them as "the French—this uncertain, unstable, and inconsistent people."

6:

The Land

France lies farther to the west than any other country on the continent of Europe except Spain. And except for Russia, it is also the largest of those countries. Yet it covers only 213,000 square miles. That is about four fifths the size of Texas.

A map of France is easy to draw because the country is hexagonal—six-sided—in shape. Along those six sides lie an ocean, two different seas, a narrow channel, and six other countries.

Five of the countries form the eastern border of France. At the north is Belgium. Then, moving toward the south, come Luxembourg, West Germany, Switzerland, and Italy. The sixth nation which adjoins French soil is Spain, at the southwest corner of the hexagon.

The southern coast of France, between Spain and Italy, is washed by the blue waters of the Mediterranean Sea. Along the western coast, north of the Spanish border, the breakers of the Bay of Biscay, which is part of the Atlantic Ocean, beat against the French shore.

But those waves are tame compared to the choppy waters of the English Channel. The Channel, at the north of France, separates that country from Great Britain.

At the northeastern tip of France, near the city of Dunkirk, the English Channel broadens, becoming the North Sea. Across the North Sea lie the Scandinavian countries.

France is a country of mountain ranges and broad plateaus, crisscrossed in all directions by rivers. Three mountain ranges

In the French Alps, Mont Blanc is snow-capped all year round.

stretch along the eastern border of France. One range, the Alps, is so high that its peaks are snowcapped all year round. The slopes are great favorites for skiers, who enjoy the sport through the winter and spring, and sometimes even until July!

North of the Alps are the Jura Mountains. North of them are the Vosges Mountains, covered with forests. A fourth mountain range, the Pyrenees, marks the border between France and Spain.

France is divided by its rivers into three separate *plateaux* or river basins. Each *plateau* is rich and fertile.

The Seine, the Loire, and the Somme Rivers flow through the Seine basin, the largest of the *plateaux*. These rivers form

The Seine River basin, a broad plateau in northern France.

a natural waterway. They connect Paris with most of France, and make the city an important inland port.

The waters of the Rhône and Saône Rivers, to the east, are too swift to navigate, but they provide electric energy for the region.

The Dordogne and Garonne Rivers, in southwestern France, form the third basin. The vineyards along their banks are the source of the world's finest wines.

Most people think of the Rhine River as flowing through Germany. Instead, it forms the boundary between that country and France, and empties into the North Sea in the Netherlands. Because the Germans crossed the Rhine to invade France so often, the river was a symbol of the hatred between the two countries for many years. Today, though, it is a means of navigation as well as a source of power for both nations.

The climate of France is as varied as the landscape. Winters in the east are severe. However, along the Mediterranean coast, the winters are so mild that beaches are crowded with sunbathers in January and February.

Sometimes in the spring and fall, a fierce wind sweeps down the Rhône Valley to the Mediterranean region, blowing roofs off houses and sending people scurrying for shelter. This wind is called the mistral.

Northwestern and central France enjoy mild winters and cool summers. Temperatures range from about 37 degrees to 70 degrees.

The Mediterranean coast, with its mild climate, is a favorite winter resort.

Much rain falls on all of France. In the mountains and in the northwest, there may be a hundred inches of rain a year. Elsewhere, at least twenty-five inches of rain fall annually. The wettest seasons are late fall and early winter. However, most Frenchmen claim that August has the worst weather. That is when almost all the French take their vacations.

Although France is divided into *départements,* it is for the purpose of government. But it falls more naturally into regions or provinces. Some provinces may once have been separate kingdoms or, even earlier, the homelands of separate tribes. Others may have certain geographical boundaries, like rivers or mountain ranges. Whatever the case, every Frenchman is as proud of his province as a Texan is of his home state. If asked where he comes from, the Frenchman will name his province. "From Alsace," he might answer. Or, "From Normandy."

The population of France has grown by leaps and bounds since the Second World War. In 1968, there was great excitement in the country because the population had reached fifty million.

Almost two thirds of those French people live in cities. The largest proportion lives in Paris, which is the home of 15 percent of the entire French population. The capital grows larger every day, just as every city in France does.

7: The Cities

The growth of French cities has been spurred by the increase in population. But it has been spurred, too, by farmers who have left their land to work in factories and by laborers from poor regions moving to cities in hopes of finding greater opportunities. They are most likely to find those opportunities in Paris.

Paris is the geographical center of France. The idea that it is the center of the country in every way is so firm in the minds of the French that distances, for example, are always measured *from* Paris, rather than to it. No Frenchman would think of saying that Paris is 782 kilometres from Marseilles. He says, instead, that Marseilles is 782 kilometres from Paris.

A fine system of railroads and modern highways, as well

as canals and waterways, connects Paris with every part of France. Other parts of the country are not so fortunate, though, and people in them are bitter about it. Often one province is linked to one near it only by a route leading through the capital.

Because of this, many goods—especially foodstuffs—must be shipped to Paris to be sold in the great market there. Then they are shipped back to villages and towns only a short distance from where they were grown.

The housewife pays high prices for her meats and vegeta-

Barges on one of the thousands of canals which link the cities of France.

bles because of the cost of distributing them. The farmer must keep his prices very low, in order to sell his produce at all. Only the merchants of Paris really benefit.

Besides being the geographical center of France, Paris is the financial, political, and cultural heart of the country. As the capital city, it is the seat of the government, and the president has his official residence there. The Senate and the National Assembly meet in Paris, and cabinet members have their offices in the city. Government buildings, in which scores of thousands of civil servants are employed, are located in Paris.

Almost all foreign countries maintain either embassies or consulates in Paris. The city is often the site of important diplomatic conferences. It was in Paris that representatives of the United States, Saigon, and Hanoi decided to negotiate the end of the war in Vietnam. Many international agencies, like UNESCO, have headquarters in the French capital.

The main offices of the great French banks are scattered throughout Paris. Many foreign banks have opened branch offices there, since Paris is the home of the *Bourse*—the French stock exchange.

Thousands of people work directly for the foreign banks and embassies. They may be top directors or important diplomats, or they may serve as secretaries, clerks, and interpreters. Many are French citizens, but they, like the others, are paid in foreign currencies. The American dollars, English pounds, and German marks they earn soon go into the pockets of hotelkeepers, restaurant owners, and merchants, as well as of maids, cooks, and chauffeurs.

Tourists, too, support these service trades, as they are called. Hundreds of thousands of them flock to Paris each year, drawn there by the beauty of the city, the glittering entertainment it offers, its luxurious shops, and its long tradition of culture.

Paris boasts the greatest art museum in the world, the Louvre. Although it covers twenty-four blocks, it is not nearly large enough for the many art treasures of the city. They can be seen, though, in the scores of other museums run by the state.

There are two opera houses in Paris, open all year round. There are half a dozen concert halls, and more than fifty theaters where plays, ranging from the great French classics to the very modern, are performed.

Paris attracts many people because it is so beautiful. It is a city of great, open spaces, where streets are broad and lined with shade trees. Parks are everywhere. Some are large and superbly landscaped, with formal gardens where flowers bloom all year round. Others are only pocket-sized, with tangles of trees and shrubs and benches where visitors can relax.

The River Seine runs through the heart of Paris, dividing it into the part known as the Right Bank and that called the Left Bank. In both sections there are magnificent monuments like that in the Place de la Concorde with its splash-

A sightseeing boat cruises up the River Seine towards the oldest and most picturesque part of Paris, the Ile de la Cité.

ing fountains or the ancient cathedral of Notre-Dame. Perhaps the most famous of all Paris monuments is the Eiffel Tower, which was the tallest building in the world when it was built in 1889.

Along the Seine, at the edge of the city and spilling over into the suburbs, are large factories. Automobiles as well as airplanes are made there. Smaller factories turn out porcelains, fabrics, and women's accessories like gloves and hand-

The Eiffel Tower, the most famous of all Paris monuments.

bags, and are located in Paris proper as well as in the suburbs.

Together they make the French capital an important industrial city. Although Paris is inland, the River Seine and a series of canals make Paris, with her population of more than 8,000,000, one of the greatest inland ports of Europe.

France's most important seaport is Marseilles. With a population of more than 900,000, it is the third largest city

of France. Its harbor, on the Mediterranean, is one of the finest in the world.

At the time Paris was founded, over two thousand years ago, Marseilles was already a thriving city. Six hundred years earlier, the Greeks had settled there, at the edge of the water. Gradually, as the town grew, it spread out into the high hills overlooking the sparkling sea.

Today, the docks of Marseilles are alive and bustling as

The harbor of Marseilles with a general view of the city.

ships are loaded with cargoes of machinery, tools, and foodstuffs. The products are sent to North and West Africa, and to the Middle and Far East as well. Passenger boats sail from Marseilles, carrying travelers to these distant parts of the world, too.

Ships returning to Marseilles most often bring cargoes of oil from the Middle East. It is refined in one of the vast plants near the city, then shipped via pipelines to northern French cities as well as to cities in Germany.

Much of Marseilles, including the old houses which made the city attractive to tourists, was destroyed in the Second World War. New ones have been built to replace them. Among them is the very modern block of apartment houses designed by the great Swiss-born architect, Le Corbusier. It is set among palm trees and overlooks the sunlit sea. The building is a model of beautiful and efficient housing for all the world.

Lyons, halfway between Marseilles and Paris, is the second largest city of France. It has a population of slightly more than one million.

In the days of the Romans, Lyons was the capital of Gaul. Even in the fifteenth and sixteenth centuries, it was a rich trading center, more important than Paris.

Today, in spite of its large population, Lyons is a quiet town, set between two hills. Two rivers, the great Rhône and the smaller Saône, flow through the city. The people of Lyons are said to enjoy the best cooking in all of France.

The modern apartment house in Marseilles which was designed by the famous architect, Le Courbusier.

Chemicals, machinery, and automobiles are all manufactured in Lyons. But, above all, she is a city of silk.

The finest silks, as well as rayons and nylons, in all the world, are spun, dyed, and woven there. Muslins, embroideries, and ribbons are made in towns nearby. They are not mass-produced, like textiles in England or the United States, and are therefore very expensive. But there is a steady demand for them, because they are beautifully designed and woven with the greatest skill.

Although Lyons is a thriving industrial city, it still retains the charm of a small town.

8:

City Life

Jean-Pierre Joubert, his sister Michelle, and his little brother Jacques live in an old section of Paris. Their apartment is on the fifth floor of a seven-story building, built of blocks of gray stone, which is more than a hundred years old. That is new for this district, though, where some buildings were put up two or even three hundred years ago.

The Joubert apartment has a small kitchen, a living room, and two bedrooms. Monsieur and Madame Joubert use one bedroom and the two boys share the other. Michelle sleeps on a folding bed in the living room.

There is a big table in the living room where the Jouberts eat all their meals. Every night after dinner, the children do their homework at the same table, while Mme. Joubert

A worker's family eats their meals in the living room.

washes the dishes. Sometimes, then, M. Joubert turns on the television set which is also in the living room. Sometimes, though, he goes to a nearby café to drink a glass of wine with his friends.

The Jouberts have often talked of moving to a larger apartment in a housing project built with government aid, just outside Paris. There are hundreds of such projects near the capital, as well as hundreds of others outside every major city in France.

The Jouberts have decided against such a move, although there will soon be a *Métro* (subway) connecting the project with the center of Paris. They still prefer to live near the workshop where M. Joubert is employed as a carpenter. He is a skilled workman and is foreman of the shop, with seven men under him.

He has made the apartment convenient for Mme. Joubert by building shelves and cabinets for her kitchen like those he makes for clients. Because there are no closets in the apartment, M. Joubert also built a large *armoire* (wardrobe). And with the help of a friend, who is a plumber, he even installed a bathroom.

When the bathroom was finished, M. Joubert bought a washing machine for his wife. Until then, she did all the laundry in the kitchen, scrubbing clothes on a board, then boiling them in a tin tub set on the gas stove.

Aside from an electric iron, Mme. Joubert's only modern appliance is a sewing machine. She uses it to make her own

A cabinetmaker at work in a small factory. M. Joubert does the same kind of work.

clothes and those for Michelle. And it helps her to keep up with the mending. Like most Frenchwomen, Mme. Joubert is expert at patching, darning, and "making do."

The Jouberts plan to buy a refrigerator soon. Now Mme. Joubert must keep perishable food on shelves under the kitchen window. But she rarely has perishable food on hand, because she markets every day, buying just what is needed.

Mme. Joubert shops at an open-air market near her apartment. She always compares prices before she buys, choosing tomatoes from one stand where they are a bargain, carrots at another. She selects meat at a butcher's stall, then stops at a different stall for butter, eggs, and milk. She goes to an *épicerie* (grocery) for sugar, rice, and the coffee she will grind herself. On her way home, she buys a small bunch of flowers.

Occasionally, Mme. Joubert goes to one of the new supermarkets. But she thinks their fruits and vegetables are not as fresh as those in outdoor markets. She has tried the few frozen foods they sell, but says they have no flavor. As for canned goods, she finds them too expensive.

M. Joubert, like the children, comes home for lunch, the big meal of the day. It begins with a spicy first course. Sometimes it is sliced sausage. At other times it is highly seasoned raw vegetables. Then Mme. Joubert serves meat or fish along

Mme. Joubert shops at a market similar to this one.

with potatoes. Either a cooked vegetable or a salad follows. After that, the Jouberts eat cheese and fruit. Everyone drinks wine or beer; for the children, the wine is mixed with water.

Throughout lunch, everyone eats the fresh bread Jean-Pierre brings from the bakery when he comes from school. Sometimes it is still hot enough to burn his fingers. He is also the one who runs downstairs to buy bread for breakfast. Mme. Joubert breaks it into large chunks, splits them, and spreads them with butter. These *tartines,* along with hot chocolate or coffee mixed with milk, are the regular breakfast of most French people.

On Sundays, they may have crescent-shaped rolls instead of *tartines.* Mme. Joubert goes to market that morning, too. She buys food for the rest of the day, as well as for Monday, when stores are closed. She usually brings home something special as well. Often it is pastry for dessert.

After dinner, in good weather, the family goes for a walk. Later they sit in an outdoor café, where the children have ice cream while their parents drink coffee or wine.

In bad weather, though, they stay indoors. The children play with their few toys or watch television. M. Joubert reads a newspaper which is only about sports. He and Jean-Pierre discuss the *Tour de France,* the bicycle race which is as important to the French as the World Series is to Americans. Mme. Joubert darns a sock or knits.

M. Joubert enjoys Sunday, his day of rest. Five days a week he works hard at his job. Recently he has been earn-

A baker's wife delivers bread. Jean-Pierre brings fresh bread from the bakery on his way home from school.

The Tour de France bicycle race is as important to the French as the World Series is to Americans.

ing extra money by working on Saturdays for M. Bineau, who lives in an apartment at the front of the building.

Once Jean-Pierre went there to deliver a message to his father. Although there is an elevator, Jean-Pierre climbed the stairway which is meant to be used by servants and tradespeople. After he had given his father the message, Bernadette, the cook, let him see the whole apartment.

Later, wide-eyed with wonder, he told his mother about it. "Seven rooms! And each of them is enormous! And all but the kitchen have fireplaces. And Bernadette has her own room, on the seventh floor." He remembers the Bineau maid and adds, "So does Françoise."

He tells Mme. Joubert about the furniture and silver, which Françoise says must be polished almost every day, and about the telephone, a luxury the Jouberts never even dream of. But Mme. Joubert wants to know about the kitchen. "It must be very modern," she says wistfully, thinking of the ads for refrigerators, dishwashers, and marvelous stoves she has seen in a women's magazine.

But the Bineau kitchen is old, dingy, and hardly better equipped than Mme. Joubert's. The refrigerator is dollhouse size. But it is adequate since Bernadette, like Mme. Joubert, does the marketing each day. Mme. Bineau does not need a washing machine because Françoise is willing to do the laundry in the kitchen sink.

Mme. Bineau claims that servants like Bernadette and Françoise are difficult to find these days. Moreover, she must pay them more each year. But for the moment, she is content with them. They perform the household tasks and leave Mme. Bineau free for her family.

She encourages her teen-age children, Denise and Alain, to bring their friends home. Once a week, she invites them all to a buffet lunch.

From time to time, she and M. Bineau go to the theater

with their children. They also go to concerts, museums, and art galleries. M. Bineau, who is an architect, likes nothing better than to stroll through the narrow streets of the Latin Quarter, pointing out to both children the beauty of the ancient buildings.

The Bineau family, like most of those of the middle class, has a car. They have just bought a small country place where they spend weekends. Mme. Bineau prides herself on being well-dressed and well-groomed. This takes up a great deal of her time, but her husband is pleased by her appearance, so she feels it is worthwhlie.

Sometimes, when M. Joubert sees the Bineau family, he wishes that he could provide a better life for his own. Yet life could be worse, he tells himself, thinking about his social security, the pensions he will have, his free medical care. He need not worry about providing for his children, as his father did. For that he is grateful.

9: School and Holidays

All three Joubert children go to school. Jacques is still at the *école maternelle* (kindergarten) but he has already learned to read.

There are both boys and girls at Jacques's school. At Michelle's primary school there are only girls and only boys at Jean-Pierre's *lycée* (secondary school).

When Michelle is eleven and has finished the seventh grade at her primary school, she will go to a *lycée* for girls. There she will start in the sixth grade. If she works hard, she will be promoted to the fifth grade and then to the fourth. It would be just the opposite if she were in an American school.

Under French law, all children must attend school from the time they are six until they are sixteen. But the law is very new, and there are not enough school buildings for older boys and girls. So, many of them leave school when they are fourteen, as was done in the past.

Education is a serious matter in France. Anyone who wants to go to a university or even to qualify for a good job, must pass his *baccalauréat*, or *bac*, when he is eighteen. The *baccalauréat* is the most difficult school examination in the world, and a great many who take it fail.

Boys and girls who want to follow a trade take a different

Under French law, all children must attend school from the time they are six until they are sixteen.

examination when they are fourteen. Then they go on to a technical school.

There are many private schools in France, where tuition is charged, but state schools are free. However, students must buy their own books. Those who cannot afford to are usually given a scholarship.

Jean-Pierre is twelve and would like an office job when he is old enough to work. So he is taking the course which leads to the *bac*. He studies many of the subjects a twelve-year-old American would: history, geography, grammar, spelling, and arithmetic. Next year he will begin German. By the time Jean-Pierre is fourteen, he will add philosophy, a science, drawing, and music to his courses.

Like all French children, Jean-Pierre does not have classes on Thursday, but he makes up for it by going to school on Saturday. His classes start at eight thirty in the morning and last until twelve. After a two-hour break for lunch, he goes back to school until four thirty. Sometimes he stops on his way home to play marbles with his friends. Not often, though; Jean-Pierre has too much homework to do.

The school each Joubert child attends is overcrowded. France is so short of schools that children everywhere have to share desks and equipment. Classes are so large that parents, as well as teachers, complain. Still, those classes grow, as the population increases.

The situation is even worse in the universities. There, students are lucky to find any place at all in a classroom. Many

A class at the law school of the University of Paris.

of them listen to the lectures of their professors over loud-speakers which are set up in the halls of the university buildings; others sit under open windows, hoping to hear what goes on in the classroom. In some cases, students can do no more than buy the notebooks of the more fortunate ones.

Some new universities have been built, but there still are not nearly enough. For a while, the government tried to solve the school problem by making the *baccalauréat* more difficult. Certain cabinet members argued that if they did so, only a few students could pass it. There would, of course, be plenty of room in the universities for those few.

But the young French were against such a solution, as they made plain when they revolted against the government in 1968. Since then, French leaders have agreed that their country needs more universities, not fewer students. They are building new ones now, and revising the course of studies, too. That way, more children of the working class will have a chance for higher education.

During the school year, French children have little time for anything but their studies. Both Jean-Pierre and Michelle must do homework every night in special notebooks. Mme. Joubert has to sign the notebooks, to show she is aware of the children's progress. Only little Jacques has time to play. Is it any wonder that the whole Joubert family looks forward to vacations?

The longest school vacation is in the summer, from the end of June until September. Because there are no real playgrounds in Paris, Jean-Pierre, Jacques, and Michelle go to the day camps run by the Paris City Council, which governs the capital. They play soccer, volley ball, and other outdoor games, and may even learn to swim. But in August, when M. Joubert has the month off, the family visits Mme. Joubert's parents at their farm in Normandy.

After his three-week Christmas vacation, Jean-Pierre will

spend another three weeks in the mountains with his class. Their trip is organized and paid for by the Ministry of Education, which is part of the national government.

The children stay together in a huge, rustic lodge. In the early morning, and the late afternoon when the sun has gone down, they go to class, just as they would if they were in Paris. But during the day, they have ski lessons, or go ice-skating or sledding on the snowy slopes. Jean-Pierre will spend both Christmas and New Year's at home, though. They are the most important holidays of the year.

At Christmas time, the children set up a *crêche*—a tiny manger made of straw, with plaster figures of the Infant Jesus, Mary, Joseph, and the Three Wise Men. On Christmas

University students march to protest government policy.

During a government-sponsored vacation, children play in the snow between classes.

Eve, Mme. Joubert's parents, who have come to Paris for the holiday, go to midnight Mass at one of the cathedrals. When they return, the whole family celebrates with a midnight supper.

What a feast they have—fresh oysters, then roast goose stuffed with chestnuts; for dessert there is a Yule log made of cake! Except for the midnight supper of New Year's Eve, it is the best meal of the year.

Little Jacques stays up with the rest of the family, although he can barely keep his eyes open. But he is not too tired to find a shoe and put it out for Père Noel (Father Christmas) to fill with gifts while he sleeps.

On New Year's Eve, the children also stay up late. They spend the day itself visiting friends and relatives, to whom they often take gifts. Twelve days after Christmas, they celebrate another holiday, the Feast of the Epiphany. A special cake with a tiny doll hidden inside is served. Whoever finds the doll in his portion is king for that day, and everyone else must do as he says.

Most French holidays are religious ones. Of those which are not, the most important is Labor Day, on the first of May. No one goes to work that day. All shops are closed, newspapers are not published, and the workers parade in every city.

The first of May is also the traditional May Day festival, when French people send bouquets of lilies of the valley to all their friends. The night before, many children go to nearby woods to pick the flowers, then sell them on street corners on May Day. The lilies are a symbol of good luck, like four-leaf clovers.

All holidays, religious or not, are the occasion for family get-togethers. That, in France, means they are also a reason for extra-special meals.

10: The Fertile Soil

How rich France is! Her soil is fertile enough to produce food for all her people. And there is plenty to spare for her neighbors.

Fifteen percent of the French people are farmers who cultivate one third of the country. On that land they grow wheat, vegetables, fruits, grapes for wine, and sugar beets, along with rice, corn, and barley.

Another quarter of French land is used for raising beef and dairy cattle. France produces more milk than any other country in the world. Much of it is made into butter. Even more, though, is made into cheese—more than three hundred different kinds.

French farmers raise pigs and sheep, along with cattle.

There is enough lamb and pork to go around, but Frenchmen love their *bifteck* (beefsteak) so much that they sometimes have to import it.

In the north of France, where the land is especially rich, many farmers have tractors and other modern equipment. Sometimes, when their farms are small, they join cooperatives and share both the cost of machinery and the use of it.

But the farmers of France face many difficult problems. Many farms are too small to be profitable. Some are no more than three or four acres. Larger farms are often made up of small strips of land, scattered around the countryside. Farmers spend much of their time traveling from one strip to another. Now, though, they are beginning to exchange separated fields for those which are side by side. Their farms

On a small farm, peasants use oxen to plow their fields which are in front of a modern chemical plant.

are beginning to look like real farms, instead of patchwork quilts.

The farmers who grow grapes for the wines of average quality often suffer great hardships. Many of them raise only grapes, and if the crops fail, they have no income at all.

On the other hand, when the weather is especially good, more of such average-quality wine is produced than the French can either drink or export. Then the farmer must sell his crop for very little, just to get rid of it. Even in good years, he may go into debt!

However, those who produce the finest wines never need to worry. Such wines are so much in demand that there is never enough to go around, so growers can charge as much as they want. If they lose their crops in bad years, they increase their prices in good years and make up for their losses.

For many of the farmers of the south, where the land is often worn out, there are no good years at all. Today the government urges those farmers to move to cities or to regions where they can find factory jobs.

Life is difficult for farmers even in prosperous parts of France like Alsace, where Yves and Catherine Rolain cultivate the fourteen acres he inherited from his father. They grow fruits and vegetables which they sell to a wholesale dealer in Strasbourg, the most important city of Alsace. The dealer sells them to the local markets or sends them by truck to cities in Germany and Switzerland.

Workers have drawn the wine from its storage casks to sample the first wine of the season.

The Rolains grow hops for brewing beer, grapes for wine, and animal fodder. They have a horse, a couple of cows, a few pigs, some chickens, and a flock of geese. Except for such staples as coffee, sugar, and salt, and for clothes and household articles like pots and pans, which they cannot make themselves, the Rolains' farm provides all they need. The few additional necessities are bought on the weekly shopping trip to the nearby village.

The Rolains get up before dawn, for a breakfast of a hearty vegetable soup, made rich with slabs of bacon. With it, they eat hunks of bread. Then M. Rolain sets off for the fields, where he will work all day.

Mme. Rolain is as busy as her husband Yves. She carries his lunch to him in the fields and sometimes works there beside him. In addition, she milks the cows and cares for the rest of the livestock. She makes butter and cheese, but no longer bakes bread, since a baker drives through the village selling it twice a week. But she cooks and cleans and does the family washing in a stone tub.

A farm woman churns her own butter.

The Rolain children help with the farm chores, too. Even Mme. Rolain's old father, who lives with them, goes out to gather firewood when the weather is good.

Day after day, this life goes on. There is a break in the routine on Sundays, when Mme. Rolain and the children go to church. Mme. Rolain pays little attention to the service, but she enjoys the chance to gossip when it is over.

There is a break in routine, too, on the important holidays, like Christmas, Easter, and New Year's. But to the Rolain children, the most exciting event of the year is the fair held in the village when the harvest is in.

Although Alsatians, like most French people, usually dress in modern clothing, they wear their traditional costumes to the fair. The women have bright, tight-laced bodices, colorful skirts, and beribboned aprons. On their heads are huge black bows, like enormous butterflies. The men wear bright red vests, trimmed with rows of gold buttons.

At the fair they dance to the tunes of an accordion and a violin. Acrobats and magicians perform their amazing feats. But Catherine and Yves Rolain are most amazed by the amount of supper their young son Hansi manages to eat.

He helps himself from a table loaded with all the Alsatian specialities. First among them is a heaping platter of sauerkraut, cooked with potatoes, thick slices of ham, pork chops, and plump, peppery sausages. Sometimes this *choucroute* is served with pheasant or duck, instead of pork. Because the fair is a special occasion, a bottle of champagne is poured

An Alsatian couple dressed in their traditional costumes.

over the dish and set aflame before it is served. With the *choucroute,* the people of Alsace drink either the excellent local wine or the equally good beer.

For dessert there is a cherry tart and a cake called *Kugelhopf,* rich with raisins and nuts. There will be other kinds of sausage, too, as well as a variety of meat pastes. But *paté de foie gras* (goose liver paste) which is produced in Alsace, will not be among them. It is far too expensive for Alsatian farmers.

Goose liver, like certain kinds of mushrooms, cheeses, champagne, and brandy, is a luxury food which comes only from France. Such delicacies are shipped throughout the world—often by plane, if they are fresh—to the tables of those who can afford them. They account for a fair share of French food exports.

More ordinary foods, though, make up the bulk of those exports. Fine wines, other than champagne, are first among them. After wines come wheat, sugar, meat, fruits, and vegetables. Flowers, which are grown in the south of France, are flown to all parts of Europe, even during the winter months.

France sells most of her garden produce to the countries of northern Europe, and especially to Germany. Trucks loaded with peas and beans, carrots and cauliflowers roll across French borders in a steady stream. Meats, too, are shipped by truck to most of northern Europe.

Dried fruits and canned fruits and vegetables are sent by boat from Marseilles to the countries of North and West

Africa, and to the Middle East. Wheat and sugar are sent both to Europe and Africa.

The market for French produce expands every year, largely because of its very high quality.

11:

In the Mines and in the Factories

Great riches lie beneath the fertile top soil of France. They make her one of the largest producers of metals and minerals in Europe. Ten percent of the world's output of sulfur, which is used to make rubber, steel, and explosives, comes from the country. France produces almost as much bauxite which is used to make aluminum. The mineral even gets its name "bauxite" from the town of Les Baux where most of it is mined.

In the northeast of France, there are large fields of both coal and iron ore. French coal, though, is of poor quality and cannot be used to produce electricity. Therefore it is turned into artificial fertilizers.

French iron ore, too, is of poor quality. But a way to purify

Workers drill for oil in central France.

it has been found, and today France is one of the largest producers of iron ore in the world. Much of it is shipped to Germany, Holland, and Belgium. But much remains in France, and is made into steel.

France also has great forests, which cover nearly thirty million acres of land. Thousands of Frenchmen work as lumberjacks, cutting down trees. Others work in sawmills where wood is cut into timber. Still others work in the plants where wood pulp is turned into all the paper France needs.

Vast fields of natural gas have been found, and there is crude oil in the south, as well. And there is further treasure in the rivers and coastal waters of the country. Fish are abundant in both. In the north, the people of Brittany bring

The interior of a coal mine in Provence.

in large catches of cod and mackerel. In the south, the Basque people fish for tuna and sardines. Seafood is packed in ice and shipped, fresh, by train and truck to all of France. When it is canned, dried, or salted, it goes to continental or overseas markets.

Although both the Bretons and the Basques are fishermen, they are far different from one another. The people of Brittany are the most religious in all of France. They often march to the sea in a *pardon* (a religious procession) to have their fishing boats blessed before they set sail in them. They are serious and stern, and their traditional costumes are black suits for men and black dresses, with white aprons and white starched lace headdresses, for women.

The Basque people, on the other hand, seem as sunny as the southern sky above them. They love to dance, and their colorful traditional dress is splashed with red or green. The men wear the famous Basque beret, which is often scarlet to match the sashes at their waists.

French waters provide energy to run French factories, as well as food for French tables. To create electricity dams have been built across the swiftest rivers in the country. In 1966, a power plant was built in the sea. It was the first such plant in the world. France also has five nuclear power plants, with others planned.

French factories turn out the steel which goes into the two million automobiles manufactured there each year. Rubber, cement, and electrical equipment are produced in great quan-

A *pardon* (religious procession) in Brittany.

Basque men perform a traditional dance.

tities. Tractors and railway equipment roll off assembly lines to be used at home or shipped abroad. French-built planes roam the skies and French-built ships sail the seven seas. And they carry such French manufactured goods as chemicals, medicines, wool and textiles, leather and furniture to ports throughout the world.

Just after the Second World War, the French government nationalized, or took over, the coal industry. At that time, it was old-fashioned and expensive to operate. With the takeover, the industry was modernized and the newest equipment installed. Today, French mines are the most efficient in Europe, and France ranks ninth in the world in the production of coal.

Other industries were also nationalized by the government. Among them was the great automobile company, Renault. It was seized after the Second World War because the owners had helped the Germans. An important news agency was seized for the same reason. But many other industries are run by the government because they are considered a "public service." These include railroads, airlines, and ships. The

Workers paint cars at the government-owned Renault factory at Flins.

government even manufactures cigarettes and matches, which are sold only in state-run shops.

In the field of transportation, French trains are modern, and they always run on time. The French airline, Air France, is the third largest in the world, as well as one of the safest. But the pride of French transportation is the beautiful new luxury liner, the *France*. She was designed and built by the French government, which has also designed and built planes like the Caravelle and the Concorde.

France has six main labor unions, as well as a number of small ones, which struggle to protect workers and gain new benefits for them. The chief union is led by members of the Communist Party. The second in importance is led by the Socialists. Others are controlled by the Catholic Church. Farm workers have similar unions.

No single union in France is very strong, and only one worker in ten belongs to a union. Nevertheless, French workers enjoy many benefits.

They pay a very small share of doctors' bills and an even smaller share of the cost of medicines. Hospital care is free. A cash allowance is given parents for each child they have after the first. Large families benefit from reduced rates for gas and electricity, subway and train fares, and even for clothing for children. The difference between what the workers pay and the actual cost is made up by the state. They are entitled to sick pay and to pensions when they retire. And all enjoy a four-week paid vacation.

French workers are well cared for, and French industry is booming. Yet France has many industrial problems still to solve.

One of her greatest difficulties is the shortage of men and women of working age. Nearly two million such people were killed in the two World Wars. Between the wars, the French birth rate fell very low. This high death rate and low birth rate meant that France lost most of one whole generation. Today, the population is made up largely of people either too young or too old to work. So the burden of supporting the greatest number of French people in history rests on the shoulders of a comparative few.

Moreover, France does not make good use of the manpower she has. Just as too many of her farms are too small to be efficient, so are far too many of her factories. Most of them are family affairs which employ no more than ten or twelve workers. The profits of these factories are small, and their owners cannot afford the new machinery which would lower costs and increase output.

France is even more backward in the way she distributes her goods. The country is made up of little shops, one for every sixty inhabitants. Some are so tiny there is scarcely room for a customer to turn around. Yet even those must bring in a livelihood for at least one person. Two or three people may depend on slightly larger shops for their living. In such shops, the profit on each item has to be very high if the owner is to pay his employees and have something for himself as well.

Long ago, the government realized that France would be a poor nation unless she turned to modern methods. As one leader said, "She must be dragged into the twentieth century."

To do that, the government made loans to merchants who wanted to expand their shops and turn them into supermarkets. They lowered taxes for larger shops and stores, too.

They also encouraged people to buy and sell on credit, something unheard of a few years ago. And they made loans and gave tax benefits to small manufacturers who wanted to enlarge their plants.

It has been hard going, though. The French people are set in their ways and do not want to change. Most small storekeepers inherited their shops from their fathers and grandfathers. They are proud of them and want to keep them as they are, to pass on to their own children. They cannot see that they, as well as France, will benefit from industrialization. So most refuse the aid offered by the government. Those who have accepted such aid are slowly driving the others out of business. And the latter, being French, react in a typical French way: they march through the streets to protest.

Sometimes, too, small shopkeepers go on strike and close their shops. A few of them have bombed offices of tax collectors, and others have blocked roads with their trucks, which has led to rioting.

Many people see such signs of unrest in France today and think the country is close to anarchy. But they are quite wrong. France is going through a difficult period and is having "growing pains."

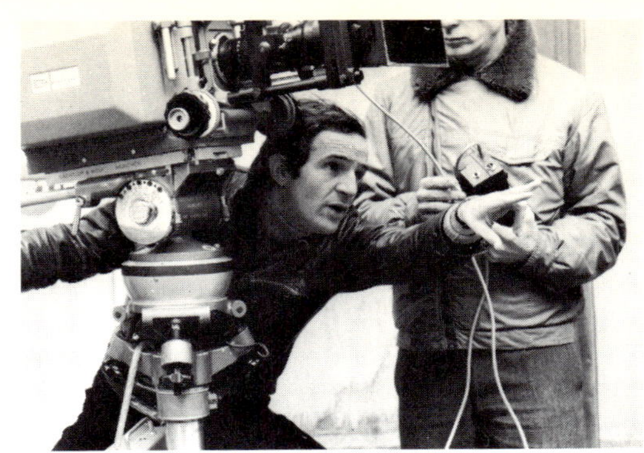

12: Artists and Artisans

In addition to her rich soil and her ores and minerals, France has another natural resource. That is the taste and talent of her people.

Many of them are artists, musicians, or writers, as many were at the time of Louis XIV. Others are superb craftsmen who now, as then, create beautiful jewels, fine furniture, and fashions. Still others are brilliant and inspiring teachers. All of them enrich the lives of those around them and bring wealth to the French treasury as well.

Long before the University of Paris was founded, in 1250, France was a center of learning. People came from all over the western world to listen to the scholars who lectured in Latin and gave the name "Latin Quarter" to the student section of Paris.

They still come, from east and west, to live in the Latin Quarter and to study literature, philosophy, painting, architecture, or music. Still others come to study in the universities in the provinces.

But the French do more than teach fine arts. They create them as well. This is especially true for paintings and sculpture, where French masters have revolutionized the whole world of art. The works of men like Cézanne, Toulouse-Lautrec, Matisse, and Pablo Picasso (who is Spanish born, but has lived most of his life in France) hang in museums throughout the world.

An important business has grown up around the French art world. In Paris, alone, there are more than three hundred art galleries. Works of the masters can be bought in these galleries, but at fantastically high prices. Works of unknown artists, who may be the masters of tomorrow, are sold for modest sums.

There are art galleries in almost every city of France as well. The best are those in the resort cities of the south, like Nice and Cannes. Moreover, paintings are sold almost everywhere. The tourist, crossing one of the bridges of the Seine, is likely to come across a painter standing before an easel, sketching the scene before him. It is just as likely that the tourist will buy the canvas, carry it home, and hang it over his fireplace. He too will be a collector of French painting, like many of the wealthiest art lovers of the world.

Paris attracts writers as often as it does painters. It is the

An artist paints a picture as he sits on one of the bridges that cross the River Seine.

center of publishing for France, where literature is so important that more than seven hundred prizes are offered to writers each year.

The majority of writers living in Paris are French. But the city is so agreeable, the atmosphere so pleasant, that others are drawn from all over the world. For the most part, the writers earn their living in their own lands, but they spend their earnings in France. Some, though, have become known as French writers. One, Samuel Beckett, an Irishman, won the Nobel Prize for his plays which were written in French.

Since the Second World War, movies have become more and more important to France, both as a form of art and a source of income. For many years after the war, the prosperity of France depended on one young movie star, Brigitte Bardot, whose films were box-office attractions throughout the world. Now, though, people in France and other countries line up outside theaters to see the work of one of the many talented young French film directors, rather than to watch a particular actor or actress. These men and women are all craftsmen of the highest order.

Other fine craftsmen design and make the fabulous jewelry which is sold to buyers who come to Paris from the four corners of the earth. Still other artisans make the superb porcelains and sparkling crystals which grace dinner tables everywhere. Some weave tapestries or restore fine old pieces of furniture to their original beauty. Hundreds of shops cater to those who want and who can afford such luxuries.

But the luxury for which Paris is most famous is her women's clothes. The workshops of the great fashion houses employ thousands of people. Twice a year, people from all over the world gather in Paris to see the new styles. Most of them are buyers for stores in other countries. They purchase original designer models, have them copied at home,

Women in the workshops of the designer Christian Dior make the clothes which will be copied throughout the world.

and then sell the copies at moderate prices. A few wealthy women buy original models to wear. Those who cannot afford dresses or suits buy handmade gloves, shoes, or handbags. If they don't buy accessories, they at least buy perfumes. All are the result of the taste and talent, combined with the hard work, of the French people.

13: Foreign Relations

As a result of the Second World War, a great change has taken place in Europe in the last twenty-five years.

There was terrible destruction during the conflict. When it was over, houses, factories, and railroads had to be rebuilt. An American aid program, the Marshall Plan, made this possible.

But far-sighted statesmen saw that new ideas were as important as new buildings. A way had to be found to avoid another war. Moreover, a plan had to be worked out so that the nations of Europe could compete with the two most powerful countries, the United States and the Soviet Union.

Each European nation was too small to become prosperous alone. Why not, these statesmen asked, do what the Americans had done nearly two hundred years earlier? Why not form a United States of Europe?

It would take many years to form such a union; it must be done step by step. But in the end, every country of Europe would benefit.

If several nations developed an industry together, they would save money by sharing costs. Moreover, such an industry could be large enough to be highly efficient, and its product would be both cheaper and better. Besides, by cooperating in this way countries would soon forget their old differences, which had so often led to war.

So the first step toward a United States of Europe was taken when the European Coal and Steel Community was formed in 1951. Its members were France, West Germany, Italy, Belgium, the Netherlands, and Luxembourg.

Among other acts, the Community swept away the currency restrictions which prevented Germany from buying the French coal she needed for steel, and France from buying the steel she needed for machinery. The result was so successful that in 1957 the members of the Coal and Steel Community teamed up to produce atomic energy to be used for peaceful purposes by each of them. That same year, they made the boldest move of all: they set up a Common Market. Its purpose was to encourage trade between European countries.

To achieve this end, the members of the Common Market, the Six as they are called, agreed on the prices of the goods they sold to one another. Often, too, they lowered duties or tariffs, or even did away with them.

It was an approach which had never been tried in Europe before, and it shocked many people. But Jean Monnet, the Frenchman who first suggested it, insisted that it would work as well on the continent as it did in the United States.

M. Monnet was soon proved right: within a few years,

Jean Monnet.

European trade increased 70 percent. At last it was possible for Frenchwomen to buy electric stoves and refrigerators at the low prices paid for them in Italy where they were manufactured. And Italian women could buy French fashions at equally low prices. Clearly, cooperation was a good idea.

Each year, the Six go a little farther toward freeing trade. Recently, they agreed on prices to be paid to farmers for agricultural products.

In the future, they hope not only to end tariffs but to do away with frontiers. They have already made it possible for citizens of the Common Market countries to cross borders without passports. Someday, those citizens will be able to live, work, and study in any of the six countries they choose.

Someday, too, England will be allowed to join the Common Market. Although she had applied for membership, she was kept out by the then French president, Charles de Gaulle. He believed that Great Britain was too much influenced by the United States. Therefore, he argued, she was not really a European country and had no place in a European organization.

The French have made a great effort to make friends with the Communist countries of eastern Europe, as well as with Communist China. They maintain diplomatic relations with all of them, and they have arranged cultural exchanges with most. French officials frequently visit the Communist countries, and the leaders of those countries are welcomed in France.

The official signing of the Franco-Soviet alliance.

France assists the Soviet Union in space exploration, scientific research, and technology. Trade between the two countries is encouraged and is increasing steadily. The French believe that such steps are necessary both for political and economic reasons.

France is on as good terms with her former colonies—Algeria, Tunisia, Morocco, and West African states like Mali and Senegal—as she is with most of Europe. These countries make up the French Community. When they were liberated, under the Fifth Republic, France guided their foreign policy and provided their defense. Now, they are completely independent.

But France has invested a great deal of money in these countries, and has lent them more to build roads and factories, schools, and hospitals. They are becoming prosperous nations on their own, with a thriving trade overseas. Much of that trade is with France.

France also has a thriving trade with Algeria, although there was great bitterness in both countries after the war in which Algeria won her independence. Since then, France has helped to rebuild the country. In return, the Algerians have given the French the right to drill for oil in the Sahara desert. They have found enough there to provide for most of France's needs. Algeria is paid well for the oil, and both nations benefit.

Just as the French have made friends with West Germany, for the good of both, they have made friends with Algeria.

14:

Special Relations: France and the United States

For nearly two hundred years, the French and the Americans were good friends. But during the Second World War, things changed.

Much of France, in those days, was occupied by the Germans. The rest was governed by an aged hero of the earlier World War, Marshal Philippe Pétain, who collaborated with the enemy. The British and Americans, like the French, looked forward to the day when France would be liberated. When that time came, a new government would have to take over. Prime Minister Winston Churchill and President Franklin Roosevelt planned one under American military control.

General de Gaulle, however, fiercely opposed the idea. He quarreled constantly with the British and Americans, but

With money from the Marshall Plan, this French farmer was able to buy and cultivate his farm.

he won the right of his people to govern themselves. However the bitterness resulting from those quarrels has lasted until today.

In spite of this, France accepted aid through the Marshall Plan. Her people were far too realistic to consider it charity. They knew that it was in the American interests to rebuild the country, in order to prevent the establishment of a Communist government.

France accepted American military aid, too, because she had no other means of defense. In 1949, she joined the North Atlantic Treaty Organization (NATO). The members of NATO pledged to help one another in case of an attack on them by the Soviet Union.

At that time, only the Americans had atomic weapons. They promised to use them to defend France if necessary. In return for this protection, the Americans were allowed to station their troops on French soil. Moreover, they were also permitted to install launching sites for nuclear weapons.

All this changed when the Soviet Union exploded an atom bomb. France, which is much closer to that country than the United States, became the first line of defense for the Americans. In case of war between the two great powers, France would have been destroyed at once.

The French were soon convinced that they would be safe only if they were independent. And they would be independent only when they had their own atomic weapons. So they set out to develop them.

They were spurred on by very real fears that American foreign policy was certain to lead to war. Besides, they resented what they considered American interference in their own affairs.

Diplomats from the United States persuaded them to retreat from a winning battle over the Suez Canal in 1956. Then, in the war with Algeria, they were humiliated when, at American insistence, the French government prevented her troops from pursuing Algerian guerillas to their sanctuaries in Tunisia. Worst of all, the Americans had sent a "goodwill mission" to end the war with Algeria, and the mission was headed by a staunch supporter of the hated Marshal Pétain. It was this "goodwill mission" which brought France so close to civil war in 1958 and brought General de Gaulle back to power.

De Gaulle was both unwilling to forgive the Americans and unable to forget the former glories of France. It was his ambition to make the country the leader of the world again, as great as she had been at the time of Charlemagne. He would use any means possible to do so, and the world situation gave him the opportunity he needed.

Since the Soviet Union and the United States seemed to be equal in military strength, power was balanced. Because each was afraid of the other, neither could move. De Gaulle saw that a "third force," even though smaller than the other two, could upset the balance. By adding its strength to one side or the other, the weakest of the three still could control policy.

So de Gaulle set out to make France such a third force.

Through trade and diplomatic missions, de Gaulle made friends with the Soviet Union and the other Communist countries. He had no need to make such an effort toward the United States. Because the Americans needed military bases in France, they were friendly to the General. So de Gaulle went out of his way to tell them when he was displeased with them.

This happened often. Sometimes General de Gaulle had real reason for his comments, as when he opposed sending American soldiers to Vietnam, since he feared it would lead to a world war. Because of this fear, he refused to renew the NATO treaty and forced allied troops to leave French territory.

But in some cases, as when he refused to admit England to the Common Market, de Gaulle seemed to act from pure spite. And no matter what his stand, he was certain to express it in the most insulting terms a chief of state could use.

Georges Pompidou, who succeeded the General as President of France, has carried on de Gaulle's foreign policy. This is especially true in the Middle East. There, in 1967, Israel attacked the Arab states. After defeating them, she occupied parts of their territories, in spite of a United Nations resolution ordering her to withdraw.

France had sold planes and other arms to Israel a few months before the war. Now, she refused to deliver them, because she believed they would be used for further aggression. She offered to return all the money Israel had paid

President Georges Pompidou of France with President Richard M. Nixon at the White House in Washington, D.C.

her. When Israel demanded the planes instead, the money was placed in a trust fund, available to Israel at any time.

On the other hand, France has shipped planes to some of the Arab countries, even though they may be used against Israel. However, President Pompidou believes this will not happen. If France supplies weapons to the Arab nations, he insists, she will have enough influence over them to prevent war. But President Pompidou is honest enough to admit that France needs oil from the Middle East. He knows that the Arab nations are more likely to sell it to France if she is on their side.

President Pompidou, like General de Gaulle, is concerned with the welfare of his own nation. He is also concerned with keeping peace throughout the world. He knows that the two go hand in hand.

He is no different from the leaders of any other country, including the United States. Each wants to do what is best for his own country; at the same time he wants to work for peace. Sometimes their ideas differ as to how this can be done, and the French and Americans become suspicious of one another and even angry. But they are certain to forget their differences soon. Both countries know that their aims are the same.

15:

Vive La France!

What is France?

To some people it is a land. To others it is a nation. Still others think of France as her people. Some see France as a civilization and as two thousand years of history. And some see France as the pleasant, leisurely way of life which has been enjoyed there for hundreds of years.

France is all of these, and all are precious to the French people. But now the French way of life is changing, and as it changes, many people fear that France, as the world has known her through the centuries, will disappear.

Yet France cannot go on as she did in the past. If the French are to live in the modern world, they must keep up with it. So today, they are seeking a means of guarding the best of their past, and combining it with the ideas and inventions of the present.

They are succeeding, but they are also creating conflicts the country has never known before. Young people rebel against their elders. New ways challenge old ones. And as methods change, traditional skills disappear.

Even the French landscape is no longer the same. Skyscrapers have gone up in Paris for the first time in its history. In the provinces, ancient cathedrals and *chateaux* stand beside modern factories.

A new France is coming into being. No one yet knows how different it will be. But those who have studied the history of the country from her early days are confident that the French people will resolve their problems, and that a greater, more glorious country will emerge.

"*Vive la France!*" they say.

"Long live France!"

Index

Photo Credits

Bibliothèque Nationale Paris: p. 10, 21, 26
Jean-Paul Cade—Christian Dior: p. 107
Commissariat Général au Tourisme: p. 8, 15; Lucien Viguier, 49; 71
Direction Générale du Tourisme: Lucien Viguier, p. 55
Documentation Française: p. 89
Allard, p. 66; Almasm, p. 38; Club Mediterranee, p. 81; Feher-Tourisme, p. 96; Holzapfel, p. 29; Le Boyer, p. 97; J. Masson-Philips, p. 78; Ministère de la Construction, p. 63; Moignard, p. 50; Pavlovsky, p. 35; Photothèque CEA, p. 86; Seneque-Tourisme, p. 105; Seraillier-Rapho, p. 68, 87; Lucien Viguier, p. 64; Windenberger, p. 39; Yan, p. 84
French Cultural Services: p. 12, 42 (upper left, lower right), 52, 69, 116
French Embassy Press & Information Division: p. 31, 33, 111, 113
French Government Tourist Office: p. 42 (upper right, lower left), 43, 46, 58, 60-61, 72, 76
Pierre Hauss—Shell Berre: p. 93
Photo Massal: p. 80
Ministère Affaires Étrangères: p. 19
New York Public Library Picture Collection: p. 17
Préfecture de la Seine: p. 58
Régie Nationale des Usines Renault: p. 98
Son et Lumière: p. 94

OGDENSBURG PUBLIC LIBRARY
0 11 03 0031492 6